OFF the Merry-Go-Round and ON with Your Life!

WORKBOOK

Power House

OFF the Merry-Go-Round and ON with Your Life!

GO FROM SPINNING TO WINNING AS YOUR NEW WAY OF LIVING

WORKBOOK

DANA MARIE ECKLUND

OFF the Merry-Go-Round and ON with Your Life!

Published by:
POWER HOUSE
An imprint of Power House Studios, LLC.
thepowerhousestudio.com

ISBN# 979-8-9853756-2-6 (Paperback) ISBN# 979-8-9853756-3-3 (eBook)
ISBN# 979-8-9853756-8-8 (Workbook) ISBN# 979-8-9853756-7-1 (Journal)

INTRODUCTION

Congratulations on choosing to get off the merry-go-rounds in your life! Now, I invite you to take steps and follow through with that decision and begin the journey that will take you from spinning to winning as your new way of living! As I state in the book, the first and most important step is to make Jesus your personal Lord and Savior. By doing this, you receive your new identity and everything you need to get off any life merry-go-round. Invite Holy Spirit into your life and let the transformation begin! (You can read more about this at the back of the companion book or on the website: OnWithYourLife.com)

This workbook is designed to use after reading the book *OFF the Merry-Go-Round and ON with Your Life!* by Dana Marie Ecklund. If you took notes in the *ON with Your Life! Journal,* then you will want to use it to help guide you through the workbook.

OFF the Merry-Go-Round and ON with Your Life! is full of Scriptures and Promises to lay hold of and personally apply to your situation. Help is here for you in God's Word as you journey off the merry-go-rounds that you have identified in your life.

Below is a list of where groups of topics are located in the book:

Scriptures dealing with unbelief	*See Chapter Three
Scriptures & prayers for children	*See Chapter Six
Steps to get off and stay off	*See Chapter Thirteen
Red-Carpet Walkway Scriptures	*See Chapter Fourteen
"In Him" Scriptures	*See Chapter Fourteen & Appendix
New Testament Personalized Prayers	*See Chapter Fourteen

Listed below are examples of different merry-go-rounds in life. This is just to name a few that I have had experience riding or been exposed to. Your list may look different, and that is totally OK. Use these and the book to help spark your thoughts as you identify, expose, and end the spinning cycles in your own life.

Our Own	**Someone Else's**
Religious & Church Going	**School Culture**
Work Environment	**Good Samaritan**
Involving Children	**Sexual Perversion**

Spouse & Marriage	Compulsive Behaviors & Addictions
Legal System	Grief & Sorrow
Fear	Survival Mode
People Pleasing	Procrastination
Lies & Deception	Depression

The workbook consists of five modules. (If you need additional modules, we suggest you pick up another copy of the workbook at the website listed below and keep moving forward!) Each module contains this same process of steps to help you get off any of your life's merry-go-rounds:

- » Identify a specific merry-go-round and its parts
- » Your personal evaluation
- » Your Red-Carpet Walkway Scriptures used to renew your mind
- » What you desire the NEW YOU to look like
- » How your thoughts about yourself are changing to look like God's thoughts about you
- » The different actions you are taking
- » How the image of yourself is changing to the image of Christ IN YOU
- » How you are resisting the urges to go back to your old way of thinking and living
- » What you are replacing the merry-go-round decoration/handlebars and desires with
- » What you are speaking to God about regarding the getting-off process
- » What God is speaking to you about this merry-go-round and your progress
- » What your life journey NOW looks like as you have gotten off the merry-go-round
- » What continued accountability you are using to stay off

Challenges will come, but you have the tools and help you need to day by day renew your mind and move forward into complete spirit, soul, and body transformation from the INSIDE out! Let us know how your journey is going! Contact us at OnWithYourLife.com and share your testimony with others!

You are equipped and loved!

Dana Marie Ecklund

OFF the Merry-Go-Round

DATE: _____

In the blank above, write THE NAME OF THE MERRY-GO-ROUND EXPOSED OR IDENTIFIED in your life. Begin with the biggest or most priority, enter the date you begin, and work through each one, revisiting this section as needed to support your progress as you get OFF the Merry-Go-Round and ON with Your Life!

COMPONENTS IDENTIFIED FOR THIS LIFE MERRY-GO-ROUND

THE CENTER POST: WHAT UNBELIEF AND LIE IS KEEPING ME ATTACHED TO THIS MERRY-GO-ROUND?

_____

WHAT FEAR IS FUELING THIS MERRY-GO-ROUND AND KEEPING IT SPINNING?

_____

THE PLATFORM/BASE: WHAT AM I DOING OVER AND OVER AGAIN THAT IS SUPPORTING THIS MERRY-GO-ROUND?

_____

DECORATIVE FIXTURES/HANDLEBARS: WHAT AM I HANGING ON TO AND LIKE SO MUCH AND DON'T WANT TO LET GO OF?

_____

THE END RESULT IF NO CHANGE IS MADE:

_____

THE END RESULT IF CHANGES ARE MADE:

_____

But clothe yourselves with the Lord Jesus Christ, and make no provision for [nor even think about gratifying] the flesh in regard to its improper desires. (Romans 13:14, AMP)

MY PERSONAL EVALUATION OF THIS LIFE MERRY-GO-ROUND

WHAT DO I LIKE ABOUT RIDING THIS MERRY-GO-ROUND?

_____

_____

WHAT DO I HATE ABOUT RIDING THIS MERRY-GO-ROUND?

_____

_____

WHY DO I WANT TO GET OFF THIS MERRY-GO-ROUND?

_____

_____

WHAT DO I SEE AS HOLDING ME BACK OR BLOCKING MY WAY FROM GOING FORWARD IN MY LIFE?

_____

_____

DO I BELIEVE I CAN GET OFF AND STAY OFF? (BE HONEST) IF NOT, EXPLAIN WHY.

_____

_____

ON THIS DAY, (INSERT THE DATE) _____

I'M CHOOSING TO STOP THE SPIN AND DO WHAT IT TAKES TO PERMANENTLY WALK OFF THIS MERRY-GO-ROUND. TODAY, I DECLARE IT, I TAKE MY FIRST STEPS OFF, AND I ENTER MY VISION OF VICTORY ON THE NEXT PAGES.

Lean on, trust in, and be confident in the Lord with all your heart and mind and do not rely on your own insight or understanding. In all your ways know, recognize, and acknowledge Him, and He will direct and make straight and plain your paths.
(Proverbs 3:5-6, AMPC)

3

MY "RED-CARPET WALKWAY" SCRIPTURES

Sanctify them by Your truth. Your word is truth.
(John 17:17)

I'M BELIEVING & CONFESSING TO PROGRESSIVELY RENEW MY MIND USING THESE SCRIPTURES:
(YOU CAN ADD MORE ALONG THE WAY.)

1. _____

2. _____

3. _____

4. _____

5. _____

6. _____

7. _____

8. _____

9. _____

10. _____

11. _____

Your word is a lamp to my feet
And a light to my path.
(Psalm 119:105, NKJV)

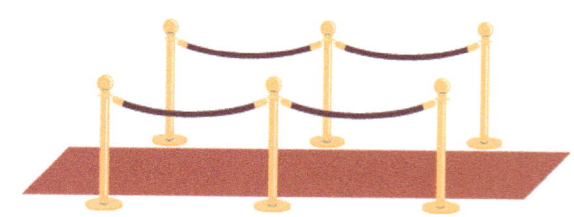

MY FORWARD MOVEMENT

WHAT I DESIRE THE NEW ME TO LOOK LIKE:
THE IMAGE I WANT TO HAVE OF MYSELF OFF THIS LIFE MERRY-GO-ROUND

_____

_____

THE DESIRES IN MY HEART I WANT TO SEE COME TO PASS:

_____

_____

HOW I WANT MY RELATIONSHIP WITH GOD TO LOOK:

_____

_____

HOW I WANT MY CHANGED LIFE TO HELP OTHERS:

_____

_____

_____

*He sends forth His word and heals them and
rescues them from the pit and destruction.*
(Psalm 107:20, AMPC)

MY FORWARD MOVEMENT

MY THOUGHTS OF MYSELF ARE BEGINNING TO LOOK LIKE GOD'S THOUGHTS FOR ME!
(RECORD ALL THE TIMES YOU NOTICE THOUGHTS OF YOURSELF CHANGING TO LINE UP AND AGREE WITH GOD'S GOOD THOUGHTS OF YOU.)

DATE & NOTES:

_____

_____

_____

DATE & NOTES:

_____

_____

_____

DATE & NOTES:

_____

_____

_____

DATE & NOTES:

_____

_____

_____

*For I know the thoughts that I think toward you, says the LORD,
thoughts of peace and not of evil, to give you a future and a hope.
(Jeremiah 29:11, NKJV)*

MY FORWARD MOVEMENT

I'M TAKING DIFFERENT ACTIONS!

(RECORD THE DATES WHEN YOU OR SOMEONE ELSE NOTICES YOU TAKING DIFFERENT ACTIONS BECAUSE YOU ARE ALLOWING CHRIST AND YOUR NEW NATURE IN HIM TO MOVE YOU FORWARD INTO A NEW WAY OF LIVING.)

DATE & NOTES: _____

_____

_____

DATE & NOTES: _____

_____

_____

DATE & NOTES: _____

_____

_____

DATE & NOTES: _____

_____

_____

I have been crucified with Christ [in Him I have shared His crucifixion]; it is no longer I who live, but Christ (the Messiah) lives in me; and the life I now live in the body I live by faith in (by adherence to and reliance on and complete trust in) the Son of God, Who loved me and gave Himself up for me.
(Galatians 2:20, AMPC)

7

MY FORWARD MOVEMENT

THE IMAGE I HAVE OF MYSELF IS CHANGING TO THE IMAGE I AM IN CHRIST!
(RECORD THE DATES WHEN YOU REALIZE THE IMAGE YOU HAVE OF YOURSELF IS CHANGING AND BECOMING RENEWED TO WHO YOU ARE ON THE INSIDE AS A BORN-AGAIN BELIEVER IN CHRIST JESUS.)

DATE & NOTES:

_____

_____

DATE & NOTES:

_____

_____

DATE & NOTES:

_____

_____

DATE & NOTES:

_____

_____

*Though our outer man is [progressively] decaying and wasting away,
yet our inner self is being [progressively] renewed day after day.*
(2 Corinthians 4:16b, AMPC)

MY FORWARD MOVEMENT

I'M RESISTING URGES TO GO BACK TO MY OLD WAY OF LIVING!

(RECORD THE DATES WHEN YOU MADE A STAND AND DEMANDED CHANGE TO COME, RESISTING AN URGE TO GO BACK INTO YOUR OLD WAYS OF DOING THINGS. WRITE DOWN IF SOMEONE ELSE NOTICED IT ALSO.)

DATE & NOTES: _____

_____

_____

DATE & NOTES: _____

_____

_____

DATE & NOTES: _____

_____

_____

DATE & NOTES: _____

_____

_____

But He gives more grace. For this reason it says:
"God resists the proud, but gives grace to the humble."
Therefore submit yourselves to God. Resist the devil, and he will flee from you.
(James 4:6-7, MEV)

MY FORWARD MOVEMENT

I AM REPLACING THIS MERRY-GO-ROUND DECORATION AND DESIRES WITH:

(RECORD EACH TIME WHEN AND HOW YOU USED GOD'S GRACE TO HELP YOU LET GO AND REPLACE NEGATIVE PATTERNS OF LIVING. RECORD WHEN YOUR DESIRES FOR THIS MERRY-GO-ROUND CHANGED AND YOU NOTICED NEW GOD-GIVEN DESIRES COMING INTO YOUR HEART.)

DATE & NOTES: _____

_____

_____

DATE & NOTES: _____

_____

_____

DATE & NOTES: _____

_____

_____

DATE & NOTES: _____

_____

_____

Let us therefore come boldly to the throne of grace,
that we may obtain mercy and find grace to help in time of need.
(Hebrews 4:16, NKJV)

Delight yourself in the Lord, and He will give you the desires of your heart.
(Psalm 37:4, MEV)

MY FORWARD MOVEMENT

WHAT I AM SPEAKING TO GOD ABOUT REGARDING THIS MERRY-GO-ROUND AND MY PROGRESS:

(WRITE DOWN THE DATES WHEN YOU TALKED TO GOD REGARDING THIS PARTICULAR MERRY-GO-ROUND AND WHAT YOU ASKED HIM ABOUT.)

DATE & NOTES: _____

_____

_____

DATE & NOTES: _____

_____

_____

DATE & NOTES: _____

_____

_____

DATE & NOTES: _____

_____

_____

Ask and it will be given to you; seek and you will find;
knock and it will be opened to you.
(Matthew 7:7, MEV)

11

MY FORWARD MOVEMENT

WHAT GOD IS SPEAKING TO ME ABOUT THIS MERRY-GO-ROUND AND MY PROGRESS:
(WRITE DOWN THE DATES WHEN YOU HEARD GOD PERSONALLY SPEAK TO YOU AND HOW HE SPECIFICALLY ANSWERED YOU ABOUT THIS PARTICULAR MERRY-GO-ROUND.)

DATE & NOTES:

_____

_____

DATE & NOTES:

_____

_____

DATE & NOTES:

_____

_____

DATE & NOTES:

_____

_____

This is what the LORD, the God of Israel says:
'Write all the words which I have spoken to you in a book."
(Jeremiah 30:2, NASB)

I'M OFF!

RECORD THE DATE WHEN YOU KNEW YOU WALKED COMPLETELY OFF THIS MERRY-GO-ROUND:

(WRITE DOWN HOW IT MAKES YOU FEEL TO BE OFF AND HOW YOU SEE YOUR LIFE NOW THAT YOU ARE NOT RIDING IT ANY LONGER. LOOK BACK IN THE SECTION WHERE YOU WROTE WHAT YOU DESIRED AND ENVISIONED THE NEW YOU TO LOOK LIKE AFTER GETTING OFF THIS MGR. DO YOU LOOK LIKE THIS NOW THAT YOU ARE OFF? I BET YOU DO!)

DATE & NOTES: _____

_____

_____

_____

_____

_____

_____

He also brought me up out of a horrible pit, out of the miry clay,
And set my feet upon a rock, and established my steps.
(Psalm 40:2, NKJV)

And I am convinced and sure of this very thing, that He Who began a good work in you will continue
until the day of Jesus Christ [right up to the time of His return], developing [that good work] and
perfecting and bringing it to full completion in you.
(Philippians 1:6, AMPC)

13

I AM IN THIS WORLD BUT ON MY PATH...
AVOIDING THE MERRY-GO-ROUND OF:

(ENTER THE NAME OF THIS LIFE MERRY-GO-ROUND)

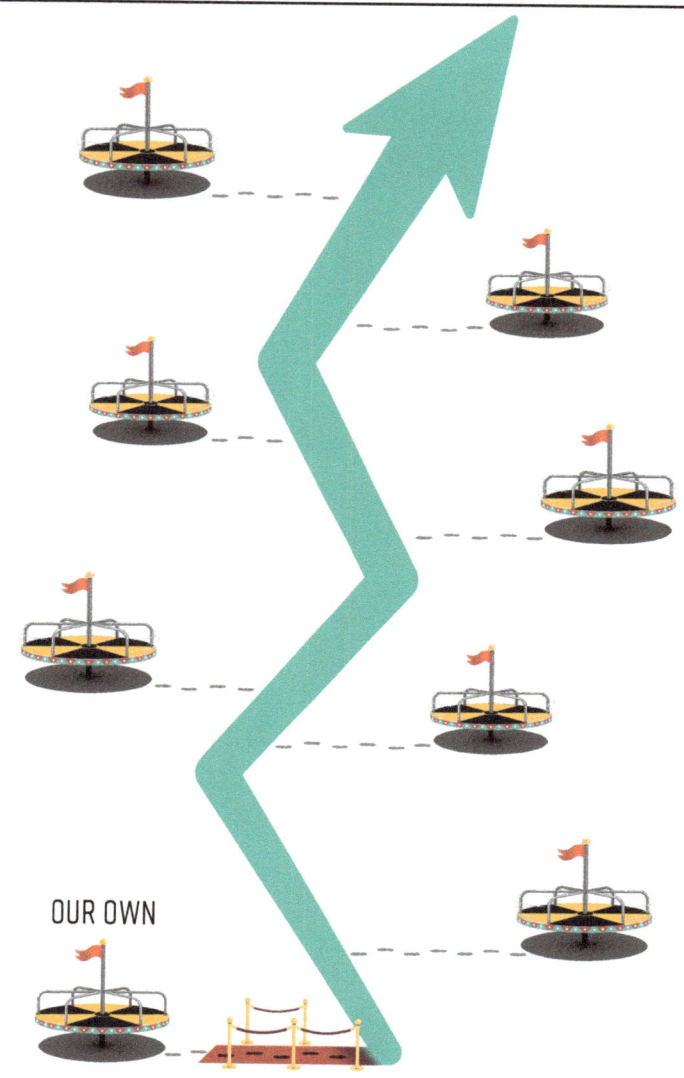

OUR OWN

Lean on, trust in, and be confident in the Lord with all your heart and mind and do not rely on your own insight or understanding. In all your ways know, recognize, and acknowledge Him, and He will direct and make straight and plain your paths.
(Proverbs 3:5-6, AMPC)

CONTINUED ACCOUNTABILITY & JOURNALING

In this section, from time to time, hold yourself accountable. Give yourself a good check-up and a reminder of where you have come from. Make sure you are still making forward progress.

Write down the dates when you come back to this workbook for review and a check-up. Journal what the thoughts, challenges, and experiences are that you have been working through.

Do you have another person holding you accountable for the progress you've made since the date you recorded getting off this merry-go-round? If so, when was it and how do they see your progress? Here are some questions to ask yourself off and on down the road: Are the old patterns of believing and acting still behind me? Am I still reaching forward to those good things which God has planned for me? (WRITE OUT PHILIPPIANS 3:13, MEV.) Am I remembering what John 5:19 says and only doing what my Good Father God leads me to do? (WRITE OUT THE VERSE.)

Be honest. Record not only your forward progress but also any relapses. Record how you got back on the merry-go-round but then got off again. Don't beat yourself up, but also don't let yourself slack off and lose the progress you worked so hard to get. You are well equipped and have been given over and above help! Regularly, take a look back at Chapters Thirteen and Fourteen in the book. It will be a good booster shot to help keep you healthy and on track! I'm cheering for you because I know that if I could do this in my life, you can do this too!

_____

_____

_____

_____

_____

_____

ON WITH YOUR *life*

_____

_____

_____

_____

_____

_____

_____

_____

_____

_____

_____

_____

Caleb silenced the people before Moses and said,
"Let us go up at once and possess it, for we are able to overcome it."
(Numbers 13:30, MEV)

ON WITH YOUR *life*

_____

_____

_____

_____

_____

_____

_____

_____

_____

_____

_____

*But when anything is exposed and reproved by the light, it is made visible and clear;
and where everything is visible and clear there is light.
(Ephesians 5:13, AMPC)*

OFF the Merry-Go-Round

_____

DATE: _____

In the blank above, write THE NAME OF THE MERRY-GO-ROUND EXPOSED OR IDENTIFIED in your life. Begin with the biggest or most priority, enter the date you begin, and work through each one, revisiting this section as needed to support your progress as you get OFF the Merry-Go-Round and ON with Your Life!

COMPONENTS IDENTIFIED FOR THIS LIFE MERRY-GO-ROUND

THE CENTER POST: WHAT UNBELIEF AND LIE IS KEEPING ME ATTACHED TO THIS MERRY-GO-ROUND?

_____

WHAT FEAR IS FUELING THIS MERRY-GO-ROUND AND KEEPING IT SPINNING?

_____

THE PLATFORM/BASE: WHAT AM I DOING OVER AND OVER AGAIN THAT IS SUPPORTING THIS MERRY-GO-ROUND?

_____

DECORATIVE FIXTURES/HANDLEBARS: WHAT AM I HANGING ON TO AND LIKE SO MUCH AND DON'T WANT TO LET GO OF?

_____

THE END RESULT IF NO CHANGE IS MADE:

_____

THE END RESULT IF CHANGES ARE MADE:

_____

_____

*But clothe yourselves with the Lord Jesus Christ,
and make no provision for [nor even think about gratifying]
the flesh in regard to its improper desires.
(Romans 13:14, AMP)*

20

MY PERSONAL EVALUATION OF THIS LIFE MERRY-GO-ROUND

WHAT DO I LIKE ABOUT RIDING THIS MERRY-GO-ROUND?

_____

_____

WHAT DO I HATE ABOUT RIDING THIS MERRY-GO-ROUND?

_____

_____

WHY DO I WANT TO GET OFF THIS MERRY-GO-ROUND?

_____

_____

WHAT DO I SEE AS HOLDING ME BACK OR BLOCKING MY WAY FROM GOING FORWARD IN MY LIFE?

_____

_____

DO I BELIEVE I CAN GET OFF AND STAY OFF? (BE HONEST) IF NOT, EXPLAIN WHY.

_____

_____

ON THIS DAY, (INSERT THE DATE) _____

I'M CHOOSING TO STOP THE SPIN AND DO WHAT IT TAKES TO PERMANENTLY WALK OFF THIS MERRY-GO-ROUND. TODAY, I DECLARE IT, I TAKE MY FIRST STEPS OFF, AND I ENTER MY VISION OF VICTORY ON THE NEXT PAGES.

Lean on, trust in, and be confident in the Lord with all your heart and mind and do not rely on your own insight or understanding. In all your ways know, recognize, and acknowledge Him, and He will direct and make straight and plain your paths.
(Proverbs 3:5-6, AMPC)

MY "RED-CARPET WALKWAY" SCRIPTURES

Sanctify them by Your truth. Your word is truth.
(John 17:17)

I'M BELIEVING & CONFESSING TO PROGRESSIVELY RENEW MY MIND USING THESE SCRIPTURES:
(YOU CAN ADD MORE ALONG THE WAY.)

1. _____

2. _____

3. _____

4. _____

5. _____

6. _____

7. _____

8. _____

9. _____

10. _____

11. _____

Your word is a lamp to my feet
And a light to my path.
(Psalm 119:105, NKJV)

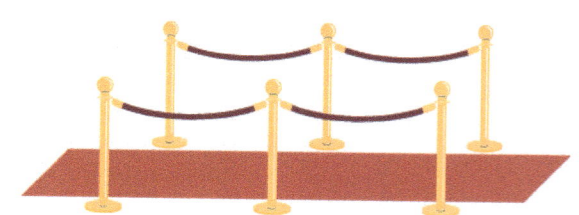

MY FORWARD MOVEMENT

WHAT I DESIRE THE NEW ME TO LOOK LIKE:
THE IMAGE I WANT TO HAVE OF MYSELF OFF THIS LIFE MERRY-GO-ROUND

_____

_____

THE DESIRES IN MY HEART I WANT TO SEE COME TO PASS:

_____

_____

HOW I WANT MY RELATIONSHIP WITH GOD TO LOOK:

_____

_____

HOW I WANT MY CHANGED LIFE TO HELP OTHERS:

_____

_____

_____

_He sends forth His word and heals them and
rescues them from the pit and destruction._
(Psalm 107:20, AMPC)

MY FORWARD MOVEMENT

MY THOUGHTS OF MYSELF ARE BEGINNING TO LOOK LIKE GOD'S THOUGHTS FOR ME!
(RECORD ALL THE TIMES YOU NOTICE THOUGHTS OF YOURSELF CHANGING TO LINE UP AND AGREE WITH GOD'S GOOD THOUGHTS OF YOU.)

DATE & NOTES: _____

_____

_____

DATE & NOTES: _____

_____

_____

DATE & NOTES: _____

_____

_____

DATE & NOTES: _____

_____

_____

*For I know the thoughts that I think toward you, says the LORD,
thoughts of peace and not of evil, to give you a future and a hope.
(Jeremiah 29:11, NKJV)*

MY FORWARD MOVEMENT

I'M TAKING DIFFERENT ACTIONS!

(RECORD THE DATES WHEN YOU OR SOMEONE ELSE NOTICES YOU TAKING DIFFERENT ACTIONS BECAUSE YOU ARE ALLOWING CHRIST AND YOUR NEW NATURE IN HIM TO MOVE YOU FORWARD INTO A NEW WAY OF LIVING.)

DATE & NOTES: _____

_____

_____

DATE & NOTES: _____

_____

_____

DATE & NOTES: _____

_____

_____

DATE & NOTES: _____

_____

_____

I have been crucified with Christ [in Him I have shared His crucifixion]; it is no longer I who live, but Christ (the Messiah) lives in me; and the life I now live in the body I live by faith in (by adherence to and reliance on and complete trust in) the Son of God, Who loved me and gave Himself up for me.
(Galatians 2:20, AMPC)

MY FORWARD MOVEMENT

THE IMAGE I HAVE OF MYSELF IS CHANGING TO THE IMAGE I AM IN CHRIST!

(RECORD THE DATES WHEN YOU REALIZE THE IMAGE YOU HAVE OF YOURSELF IS CHANGING AND BECOMING RENEWED TO WHO YOU ARE ON THE INSIDE AS A BORN-AGAIN BELIEVER IN CHRIST JESUS.)

DATE & NOTES:

_____

_____

_____

DATE & NOTES:

_____

_____

_____

DATE & NOTES:

_____

_____

_____

DATE & NOTES:

_____

_____

_____

Though our outer man is [progressively] decaying and wasting away,
yet our inner self is being [progressively] renewed day after day.
(2 Corinthians 4:16b, AMPC)

MY FORWARD MOVEMENT

I'M RESISTING URGES TO GO BACK TO MY OLD WAY OF LIVING!

(RECORD THE DATES WHEN YOU MADE A STAND AND DEMANDED CHANGE TO COME, RESISTING AN URGE TO GO BACK INTO YOUR OLD WAYS OF DOING THINGS. WRITE DOWN IF SOMEONE ELSE NOTICED IT ALSO.)

DATE & NOTES: _____

_____

_____

DATE & NOTES: _____

_____

_____

DATE & NOTES: _____

_____

_____

DATE & NOTES: _____

_____

_____

But He gives more grace. For this reason it says:
"God resists the proud, but gives grace to the humble."
Therefore submit yourselves to God. Resist the devil, and he will flee from you.
(James 4:6-7, MEV)

MY FORWARD MOVEMENT

I AM REPLACING THIS MERRY-GO-ROUND DECORATION AND DESIRES WITH:

(RECORD EACH TIME WHEN AND HOW YOU USED GOD'S GRACE TO HELP YOU LET GO AND REPLACE NEGATIVE PATTERNS OF LIVING. RECORD WHEN YOUR DESIRES FOR THIS MERRY-GO-ROUND CHANGED AND YOU NOTICED NEW GOD-GIVEN DESIRES COMING INTO YOUR HEART.)

DATE & NOTES:

_____

_____

DATE & NOTES:

_____

_____

DATE & NOTES:

_____

_____

DATE & NOTES:

_____

_____

Let us therefore come boldly to the throne of grace,
that we may obtain mercy and find grace to help in time of need.
(Hebrews 4:16, NKJV)

Delight yourself in the Lord, and He will give you the desires of your heart.
(Psalm 37:4, MEV)

MY FORWARD MOVEMENT

WHAT I AM SPEAKING TO GOD ABOUT REGARDING THIS MERRY-GO-ROUND AND MY PROGRESS:
(WRITE DOWN THE DATES WHEN YOU TALKED TO GOD REGARDING THIS PARTICULAR MERRY-GO-ROUND AND WHAT YOU ASKED HIM ABOUT.)

DATE & NOTES: _____

_____

_____

DATE & NOTES: _____

_____

_____

DATE & NOTES: _____

_____

_____

DATE & NOTES: _____

_____

_____

Ask and it will be given to you; seek and you will find;
knock and it will be opened to you.
(Matthew 7:7, MEV)

MY FORWARD MOVEMENT

WHAT GOD IS SPEAKING TO ME ABOUT THIS MERRY-GO-ROUND AND MY PROGRESS:
(WRITE DOWN THE DATES WHEN YOU HEARD GOD PERSONALLY SPEAK TO YOU AND HOW HE SPECIFICALLY ANSWERED YOU ABOUT THIS PARTICULAR MERRY-GO-ROUND.)

DATE & NOTES: _____

_____

_____

DATE & NOTES: _____

_____

_____

DATE & NOTES: _____

_____

_____

DATE & NOTES: _____

_____

_____

This is what the LORD, the God of Israel says:
'Write all the words which I have spoken to you in a book."
(Jeremiah 30:2, NASB)

I'M OFF!

RECORD THE DATE WHEN YOU KNEW YOU WALKED COMPLETELY OFF THIS MERRY-GO-ROUND:

(WRITE DOWN HOW IT MAKES YOU FEEL TO BE OFF AND HOW YOU SEE YOUR LIFE NOW THAT YOU ARE NOT RIDING IT ANY LONGER. LOOK BACK IN THE SECTION WHERE YOU WROTE WHAT YOU DESIRED AND ENVISIONED THE NEW YOU TO LOOK LIKE AFTER GETTING OFF THIS MGR. DO YOU LOOK LIKE THIS NOW THAT YOU ARE OFF? I BET YOU DO!)

DATE: _____

_____

_____

_____

_____

_____

_____

He also brought me up out of a horrible pit, out of the miry clay,
And set my feet upon a rock, and established my steps.
(Psalm 40:2, NKJV)

And I am convinced and sure of this very thing, that He Who began a good work in you will continue
until the day of Jesus Christ [right up to the time of His return], developing [that good work] and
perfecting and bringing it to full completion in you.
(Philippians 1:6, AMPC)

I AM IN THIS WORLD BUT ON MY PATH...
AVOIDING THE MERRY-GO-ROUND OF:

(ENTER THE NAME OF THIS LIFE MERRY-GO-ROUND)

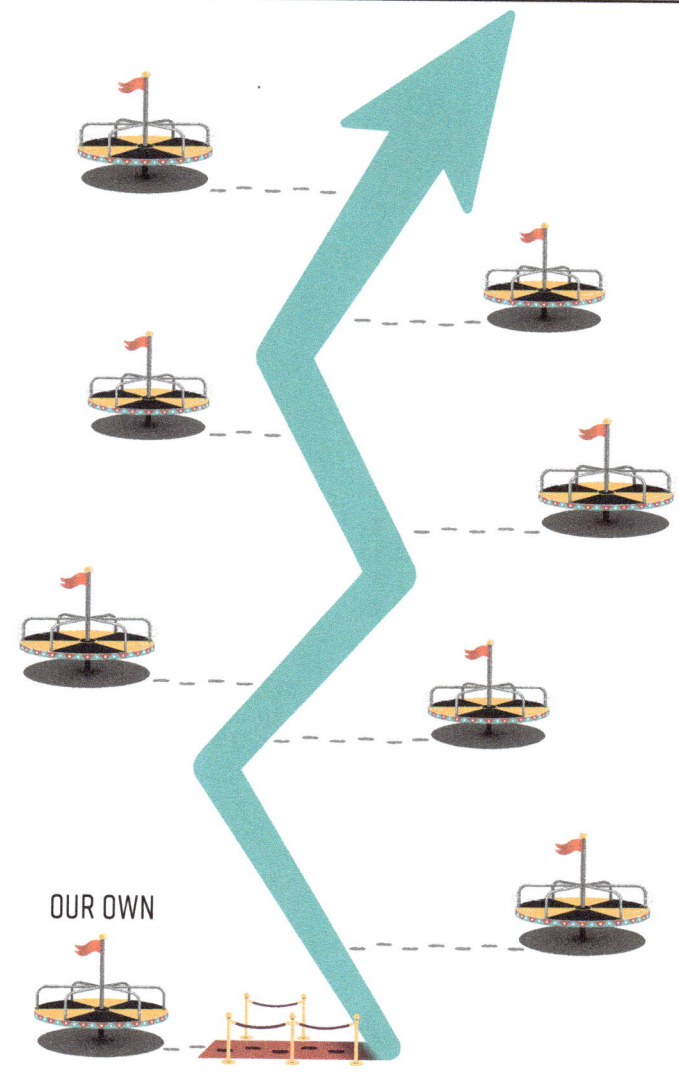

OUR OWN

Lean on, trust in, and be confident in the Lord with all your heart and mind and do not rely on your own insight or understanding. In all your ways know, recognize, and acknowledge Him, and He will direct and make straight and plain your paths.
(Proverbs 3:5-6, AMPC)

CONTINUED ACCOUNTABILITY & JOURNALING

In this section, from time to time, hold yourself accountable. Give yourself a good check-up and a reminder of where you have come from. Make sure you are still making forward progress.

Write down the dates when you come back to this workbook for review and a check-up. Journal what the thoughts, challenges, and experiences are that you have been working through.

Do you have another person holding you accountable for the progress you've made since the date you recorded getting off this merry-go-round? If so, when was it and how do they see your progress? Here are some questions to ask yourself off and on down the road: Are the old patterns of believing and acting still behind me? Am I still reaching forward to those good things which God has planned for me? (WRITE OUT PHILIPPIANS 3:13, MEV.) Am I remembering what John 5:19 says and only doing what my Good Father God leads me to do? (WRITE OUT THE VERSE.)

Be honest. Record not only your forward progress but also any relapses. Record how you got back on the merry-go-round but then got off again. Don't beat yourself up, but also don't let yourself slack off and lose the progress you worked so hard to get. You are well equipped and have been given over and above help! Regularly, take a look back at Chapters Thirteen and Fourteen in the book. It will be a good booster shot to help keep you healthy and on track! I'm cheering for you because I know that if I could do this in my life, you can do this too!

_____

_____

_____

_____

_____

_____

_____

_____

_____

_____

_____

_____

Caleb silenced the people before Moses and said,
"Let us go up at once and possess it, for we are able to overcome it."
(Numbers 13:30, MEV)

ON WITH YOUR life

_____

_____

_____

_____

_____

_____

_____

_____

_____

_____

_____

But when anything is exposed and reproved by the light, it is made visible and clear; and where everything is visible and clear there is light.
(Ephesians 5:13, AMPC)

OFF the Merry-Go-Round

DATE: _____

In the blank above, write THE NAME OF THE MERRY-GO-ROUND EXPOSED OR IDENTIFIED in your life. Begin with the biggest or most priority, enter the date you begin, and work through each one, revisiting this section as needed to support your progress as you get OFF the Merry-Go-Round and ON with Your Life!

COMPONENTS IDENTIFIED FOR THIS LIFE MERRY-GO-ROUND

THE CENTER POST: WHAT UNBELIEF AND LIE IS KEEPING ME ATTACHED TO THIS MERRY-GO-ROUND?

_____

_____

WHAT FEAR IS FUELING THIS MERRY-GO-ROUND AND KEEPING IT SPINNING?

_____

_____

THE PLATFORM/BASE: WHAT AM I DOING OVER AND OVER AGAIN THAT IS SUPPORTING THIS MERRY-GO-ROUND?

_____

_____

DECORATIVE FIXTURES/HANDLEBARS: WHAT AM I HANGING ON TO AND LIKE SO MUCH AND DON'T WANT TO LET GO OF?

_____

_____

THE END RESULT IF NO CHANGE IS MADE:

_____

_____

THE END RESULT IF CHANGES ARE MADE:

_____

_____

_____

*But clothe yourselves with the Lord Jesus Christ,
and make no provision for [nor even think about gratifying]
the flesh in regard to its improper desires.
(Romans 13:14, AMP)*

MY PERSONAL EVALUATION OF THIS LIFE MERRY-GO-ROUND

WHAT DO I LIKE ABOUT RIDING THIS MERRY-GO-ROUND?

_____

_____

WHAT DO I HATE ABOUT RIDING THIS MERRY-GO-ROUND?

_____

_____

WHY DO I WANT TO GET OFF THIS MERRY-GO-ROUND?

_____

_____

WHAT DO I SEE AS HOLDING ME BACK OR BLOCKING MY WAY FROM GOING FORWARD IN MY LIFE?

_____

_____

DO I BELIEVE I CAN GET OFF AND STAY OFF? (BE HONEST) IF NOT, EXPLAIN WHY.

_____

_____

ON THIS DAY, (INSERT THE DATE) _____

I'M CHOOSING TO STOP THE SPIN AND DO WHAT IT TAKES TO PERMANENTLY WALK OFF THIS MERRY-GO-ROUND. TODAY, I DECLARE IT, I TAKE MY FIRST STEPS OFF, AND I ENTER MY VISION OF VICTORY ON THE NEXT PAGES.

*Lean on, trust in, and be confident in the Lord with all your heart and mind and do not rely on your own insight or understanding.
In all your ways know, recognize, and acknowledge Him, and He will direct and make straight and plain your paths.*
(Proverbs 3:5-6, AMPC)

MY "RED-CARPET WALKWAY" SCRIPTURES

Sanctify them by Your truth. Your word is truth.
(John 17:17)

I'M BELIEVING & CONFESSING TO PROGRESSIVELY RENEW MY MIND USING THESE SCRIPTURES:
(YOU CAN ADD MORE ALONG THE WAY.)

1. _____

2. _____

3. _____

4. _____

5. _____

6. _____

7. _____

8. _____

9. _____

10. _____

11. _____

Your word is a lamp to my feet
And a light to my path.
(Psalm 119:105, NKJV)

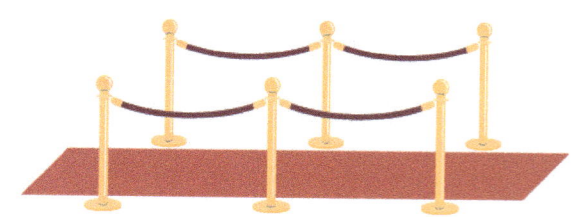

MY FORWARD MOVEMENT

WHAT I DESIRE THE NEW ME TO LOOK LIKE:
THE IMAGE I WANT TO HAVE OF MYSELF OFF THIS LIFE MERRY-GO-ROUND

_____

_____

THE DESIRES IN MY HEART I WANT TO SEE COME TO PASS:

_____

_____

HOW I WANT MY RELATIONSHIP WITH GOD TO LOOK:

_____

_____

HOW I WANT MY CHANGED LIFE TO HELP OTHERS:

_____

_____

_____

He sends forth His word and heals them and rescues them from the pit and destruction.
(Psalm 107:20, AMPC)

MY FORWARD MOVEMENT

MY THOUGHTS OF MYSELF ARE BEGINNING TO LOOK LIKE GOD'S THOUGHTS FOR ME!
(RECORD ALL THE TIMES YOU NOTICE THOUGHTS OF YOURSELF CHANGING TO LINE UP AND AGREE WITH GOD'S GOOD THOUGHTS OF YOU.)

DATE & NOTES: _____

_____

_____

DATE & NOTES: _____

_____

_____

DATE & NOTES: _____

_____

_____

DATE & NOTES: _____

_____

_____

For I know the thoughts that I think toward you, says the LORD,
thoughts of peace and not of evil, to give you a future and a hope.
(Jeremiah 29:11, NKJV)

MY FORWARD MOVEMENT

I'M TAKING DIFFERENT ACTIONS!

(RECORD THE DATES WHEN YOU OR SOMEONE ELSE NOTICES YOU TAKING DIFFERENT ACTIONS BECAUSE YOU ARE ALLOWING CHRIST AND YOUR NEW NATURE IN HIM TO MOVE YOU FORWARD INTO A NEW WAY OF LIVING.)

DATE & NOTES:

_____

_____

DATE & NOTES:

_____

_____

DATE & NOTES:

_____

_____

DATE & NOTES:

_____

_____

I have been crucified with Christ [in Him I have shared His crucifixion]; it is no longer I who live, but Christ (the Messiah) lives in me; and the life I now live in the body I live by faith in (by adherence to and reliance on and complete trust in) the Son of God, Who loved me and gave Himself up for me.
(Galatians 2:20, AMPC)

43

MY FORWARD MOVEMENT

THE IMAGE I HAVE OF MYSELF IS CHANGING TO THE IMAGE I AM IN CHRIST!

(RECORD THE DATES WHEN YOU REALIZE THE IMAGE YOU HAVE OF YOURSELF IS CHANGING AND BECOMING RENEWED TO WHO YOU ARE ON THE INSIDE AS A BORN-AGAIN BELIEVER IN CHRIST JESUS.)

DATE & NOTES: _____

_____

_____

DATE & NOTES: _____

_____

_____

DATE & NOTES: _____

_____

_____

DATE & NOTES: _____

_____

_____

Though our outer man is [progressively] decaying and wasting away,
yet our inner self is being [progressively] renewed day after day.
(2 Corinthians 4:16b, AMPC)

MY FORWARD MOVEMENT

I'M RESISTING URGES TO GO BACK TO MY OLD WAY OF LIVING!

(RECORD THE DATES WHEN YOU MADE A STAND AND DEMANDED CHANGE TO COME, RESISTING AN URGE TO GO BACK INTO YOUR OLD WAYS OF DOING THINGS. WRITE DOWN IF SOMEONE ELSE NOTICED IT ALSO.)

DATE & NOTES: _____

_____

_____

DATE & NOTES: _____

_____

_____

DATE & NOTES: _____

_____

_____

DATE & NOTES: _____

_____

_____

_____

But He gives more grace. For this reason it says:
"God resists the proud, but gives grace to the humble."
Therefore submit yourselves to God. Resist the devil, and he will flee from you.
(James 4:6-7, MEV)

MY FORWARD MOVEMENT

I AM REPLACING THIS MERRY-GO-ROUND DECORATION AND DESIRES WITH:

(RECORD EACH TIME WHEN AND HOW YOU USED GOD'S GRACE TO HELP YOU LET GO AND REPLACE NEGATIVE PATTERNS OF LIVING. RECORD WHEN YOUR DESIRES FOR THIS MERRY-GO-ROUND CHANGED AND YOU NOTICED NEW GOD-GIVEN DESIRES COMING INTO YOUR HEART.)

DATE & NOTES: _____

_____

_____

DATE & NOTES: _____

_____

_____

DATE & NOTES: _____

_____

_____

DATE & NOTES: _____

_____

_____

Let us therefore come boldly to the throne of grace,
that we may obtain mercy and find grace to help in time of need.
(Hebrews 4:16, NKJV)

Delight yourself in the Lord, and He will give you the desires of your heart.
(Psalm 37:4, MEV)

MY FORWARD MOVEMENT

WHAT I AM SPEAKING TO GOD ABOUT REGARDING THIS MERRY-GO-ROUND AND MY PROGRESS:
(WRITE DOWN THE DATES WHEN YOU TALKED TO GOD REGARDING THIS PARTICULAR MERRY-GO-ROUND AND WHAT YOU ASKED HIM ABOUT.)

DATE & NOTES: _____

_____

_____

DATE & NOTES: _____

_____

_____

DATE & NOTES: _____

_____

_____

DATE & NOTES: _____

_____

_____

Ask and it will be given to you; seek and you will find;
knock and it will be opened to you.
(Matthew 7:7, MEV)

47

MY FORWARD MOVEMENT

WHAT GOD IS SPEAKING TO ME ABOUT THIS MERRY-GO-ROUND AND MY PROGRESS:
(WRITE DOWN THE DATES WHEN YOU HEARD GOD PERSONALLY SPEAK TO YOU AND HOW HE SPECIFICALLY ANSWERED YOU ABOUT THIS PARTICULAR MERRY-GO-ROUND.)

DATE & NOTES:

_____

_____

_____

DATE & NOTES:

_____

_____

_____

DATE & NOTES:

_____

_____

_____

DATE & NOTES:

_____

_____

_____

This is what the LORD, the God of Israel says:
'Write all the words which I have spoken to you in a book."
(Jeremiah 30:2, NASB)

I'M OFF!

RECORD THE DATE WHEN YOU KNEW YOU WALKED COMPLETELY OFF THIS MERRY-GO-ROUND:

(WRITE DOWN HOW IT MAKES YOU FEEL TO BE OFF AND HOW YOU SEE YOUR LIFE NOW THAT YOU ARE NOT RIDING IT ANY LONGER. LOOK BACK IN THE SECTION WHERE YOU WROTE WHAT YOU DESIRED AND ENVISIONED THE NEW YOU TO LOOK LIKE AFTER GETTING OFF THIS MGR. DO YOU LOOK LIKE THIS NOW THAT YOU ARE OFF? I BET YOU DO!)

DATE: _____

_____

_____

_____

_____

_____

_____

_____

He also brought me up out of a horrible pit, out of the miry clay,
And set my feet upon a rock, and established my steps.
(Psalm 40:2, NKJV)

And I am convinced and sure of this very thing, that He Who began a good work in you will continue
until the day of Jesus Christ [right up to the time of His return], developing [that good work] and
perfecting and bringing it to full completion in you.
(Philippians 1:6, AMPC)

I AM IN THIS WORLD BUT ON MY PATH...
AVOIDING THE MERRY-GO-ROUND OF:

(ENTER THE NAME OF THIS LIFE MERRY-GO-ROUND)

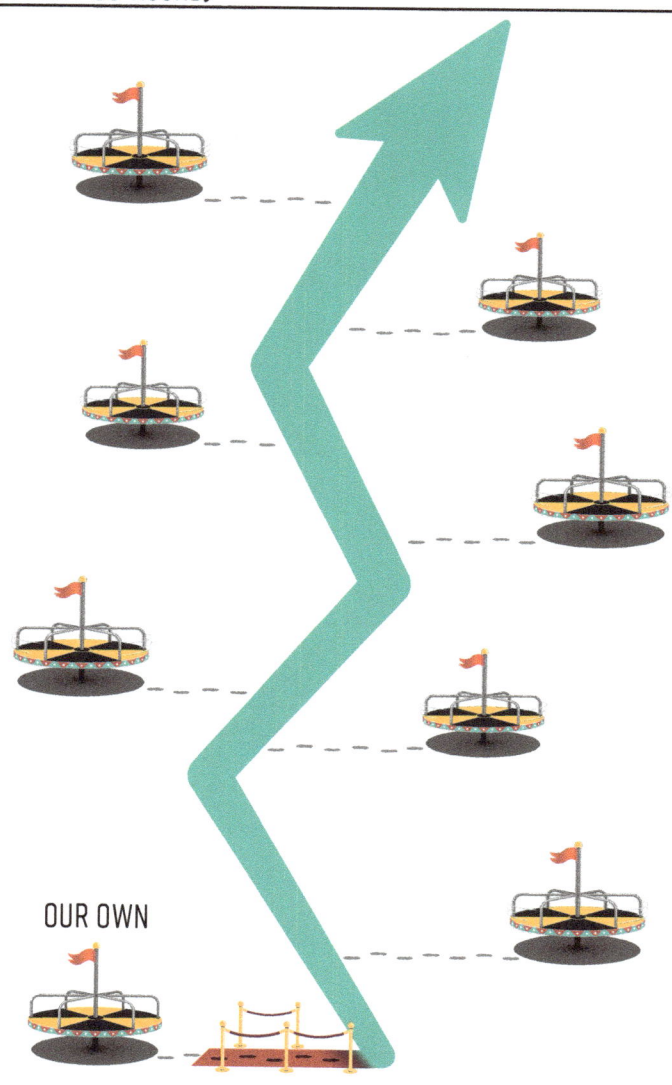

OUR OWN

Lean on, trust in, and be confident in the Lord with all your heart and mind and do not rely on your own insight or understanding. In all your ways know, recognize, and acknowledge Him, and He will direct and make straight and plain your paths.
(Proverbs 3:5-6, AMPC)

CONTINUED ACCOUNTABILITY & JOURNALING

In this section, from time to time, hold yourself accountable. Give yourself a good check-up and a reminder of where you have come from. Make sure you are still making forward progress.

Write down the dates when you come back to this workbook for review and a check-up. Journal what the thoughts, challenges, and experiences are that you have been working through.

Do you have another person holding you accountable for the progress you've made since the date you recorded getting off this merry-go-round? If so, when was it and how do they see your progress? Here are some questions to ask yourself off and on down the road: Are the old patterns of believing and acting still behind me? Am I still reaching forward to those good things which God has planned for me? (WRITE OUT PHILIPPIANS 3:13, MEV.) Am I remembering what John 5:19 says and only doing what my Good Father God leads me to do? (WRITE OUT THE VERSE.)

Be honest. Record not only your forward progress but also any relapses. Record how you got back on the merry-go-round but then got off again. Don't beat yourself up, but also don't let yourself slack off and lose the progress you worked so hard to get. You are well equipped and have been given over and above help! Regularly, take a look back at Chapters Thirteen and Fourteen in the book. It will be a good booster shot to help keep you healthy and on track! I'm cheering for you because I know that if I could do this in my life, you can do this too!

_____

_____

_____

_____

_____

_____

_____

_____

_____

_____

_____

_____

_____

_____

_____

_____

_____

_____

_____

_____

Caleb silenced the people before Moses and said,
"Let us go up at once and possess it, for we are able to overcome it."
(Numbers 13:30, MEV)

ON WITH YOUR life

But when anything is exposed and reproved by the light, it is made visible and clear; and where everything is visible and clear there is light.
(Ephesians 5:13, AMPC)

OFF the Merry-Go-Round

DATE: _____

In the blank above, write THE NAME OF THE MERRY-GO-ROUND EXPOSED OR IDENTIFIED in your life. Begin with the biggest or most priority, enter the date you begin, and work through each one, revisiting this section as needed to support your progress as you get OFF the Merry-Go-Round and ON with Your Life!

COMPONENTS IDENTIFIED FOR THIS LIFE MERRY-GO-ROUND

THE CENTER POST: WHAT UNBELIEF AND LIE IS KEEPING ME ATTACHED TO THIS MERRY-GO-ROUND?

_____

WHAT FEAR IS FUELING THIS MERRY-GO-ROUND AND KEEPING IT SPINNING?

_____

THE PLATFORM/BASE: WHAT AM I DOING OVER AND OVER AGAIN THAT IS SUPPORTING THIS MERRY-GO-ROUND?

_____

DECORATIVE FIXTURES/HANDLEBARS: WHAT AM I HANGING ON TO AND LIKE SO MUCH AND DON'T WANT TO LET GO OF?

_____

THE END RESULT IF NO CHANGE IS MADE: _____

_____

THE END RESULT IF CHANGES ARE MADE: _____

_____

_____

*But clothe yourselves with the Lord Jesus Christ,
and make no provision for [nor even think about gratifying]
the flesh in regard to its improper desires.
(Romans 13:14, AMP)*

MY PERSONAL EVALUATION OF THIS
LIFE MERRY-GO-ROUND

WHAT DO I LIKE ABOUT RIDING THIS MERRY-GO-ROUND?

_____

WHAT DO I HATE ABOUT RIDING THIS MERRY-GO-ROUND?

_____

WHY DO I WANT TO GET OFF THIS MERRY-GO-ROUND?

_____

WHAT DO I SEE AS HOLDING ME BACK OR BLOCKING MY WAY FROM GOING FORWARD IN MY LIFE?

_____

DO I BELIEVE I CAN GET OFF AND STAY OFF? (BE HONEST) IF NOT, EXPLAIN WHY.

_____

ON THIS DAY, (INSERT THE DATE) _____

I'M CHOOSING TO STOP THE SPIN AND DO WHAT IT TAKES TO PERMANENTLY WALK OFF THIS MERRY-GO-ROUND. TODAY, I DECLARE IT, I TAKE MY FIRST STEPS OFF, AND I ENTER MY VISION OF VICTORY ON THE NEXT PAGES.

Lean on, trust in, and be confident in the Lord with all your heart and mind and do not rely on your own insight or understanding. In all your ways know, recognize, and acknowledge Him, and He will direct and make straight and plain your paths.
(Proverbs 3:5-6, AMPC)

57

MY "RED-CARPET WALKWAY" SCRIPTURES

Sanctify them by Your truth. Your word is truth.
(John 17:17)

I'M BELIEVING & CONFESSING TO PROGRESSIVELY RENEW MY MIND USING THESE SCRIPTURES:
(YOU CAN ADD MORE ALONG THE WAY.)

1. _____

2. _____

3. _____

4. _____

5. _____

6. _____

7. _____

8. _____

9. _____

10. _____

11. _____

Your word is a lamp to my feet
And a light to my path.
(Psalm 119:105, NKJV)

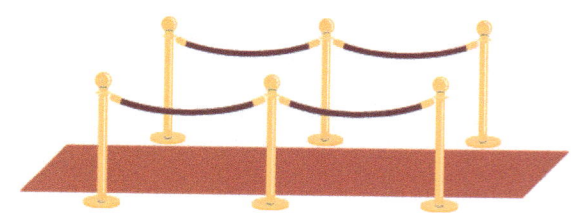

MY FORWARD MOVEMENT

WHAT I DESIRE THE NEW ME TO LOOK LIKE:
THE IMAGE I WANT TO HAVE OF MYSELF OFF THIS LIFE MERRY-GO-ROUND

_____

_____

THE DESIRES IN MY HEART I WANT TO SEE COME TO PASS:

_____

_____

HOW I WANT MY RELATIONSHIP WITH GOD TO LOOK:

_____

_____

HOW I WANT MY CHANGED LIFE TO HELP OTHERS:

_____

_____

_____

*He sends forth His word and heals them and
rescues them from the pit and destruction.
(Psalm 107:20, AMPC)*

MY FORWARD MOVEMENT

MY THOUGHTS OF MYSELF ARE BEGINNING TO LOOK LIKE GOD'S THOUGHTS FOR ME!
(RECORD ALL THE TIMES YOU NOTICE THOUGHTS OF YOURSELF CHANGING TO LINE UP AND AGREE WITH GOD'S GOOD THOUGHTS OF YOU.)

DATE & NOTES:

_____

_____

DATE & NOTES:

_____

_____

DATE & NOTES:

_____

_____

DATE & NOTES:

_____

_____

For I know the thoughts that I think toward you, says the LORD,
thoughts of peace and not of evil, to give you a future and a hope.
(Jeremiah 29:11, NKJV)

MY FORWARD MOVEMENT

I'M TAKING DIFFERENT ACTIONS!

(RECORD THE DATES WHEN YOU OR SOMEONE ELSE NOTICES YOU TAKING DIFFERENT ACTIONS BECAUSE YOU ARE ALLOWING CHRIST AND YOUR NEW NATURE IN HIM TO MOVE YOU FORWARD INTO A NEW WAY OF LIVING.)

DATE & NOTES: _____

_____

_____

DATE & NOTES: _____

_____

_____

DATE & NOTES: _____

_____

_____

DATE & NOTES: _____

_____

_____

I have been crucified with Christ [in Him I have shared His crucifixion]; it is no longer I who live, but Christ (the Messiah) lives in me; and the life I now live in the body I live by faith in (by adherence to and reliance on and complete trust in) the Son of God, Who loved me and gave Himself up for me.
(Galatians 2:20, AMPC)

MY FORWARD MOVEMENT

THE IMAGE I HAVE OF MYSELF IS CHANGING TO THE IMAGE I AM IN CHRIST!

(RECORD THE DATES WHEN YOU REALIZE THE IMAGE YOU HAVE OF YOURSELF IS CHANGING AND BECOMING RENEWED TO WHO YOU ARE ON THE INSIDE AS A BORN-AGAIN BELIEVER IN CHRIST JESUS.)

DATE & NOTES: _____

_____

_____

DATE & NOTES: _____

_____

_____

DATE & NOTES: _____

_____

_____

DATE & NOTES: _____

_____

_____

Though our outer man is [progressively] decaying and wasting away,
yet our inner self is being [progressively] renewed day after day.
(2 Corinthians 4:16b, AMPC)

MY FORWARD MOVEMENT

I'M RESISTING URGES TO GO BACK TO MY OLD WAY OF LIVING!
(RECORD THE DATES WHEN YOU MADE A STAND AND DEMANDED CHANGE TO COME, RESISTING AN URGE TO GO BACK INTO YOUR OLD WAYS OF DOING THINGS. WRITE DOWN IF SOMEONE ELSE NOTICED IT ALSO.)

DATE & NOTES: _____

_____

_____

DATE & NOTES: _____

_____

_____

DATE & NOTES: _____

_____

_____

DATE & NOTES: _____

_____

_____

But He gives more grace. For this reason it says:
"God resists the proud, but gives grace to the humble."
Therefore submit yourselves to God. Resist the devil, and he will flee from you.
(James 4:6-7, MEV)

63

MY FORWARD MOVEMENT

I AM REPLACING THIS MERRY-GO-ROUND DECORATION AND DESIRES WITH:

(RECORD EACH TIME WHEN AND HOW YOU USED GOD'S GRACE TO HELP YOU LET GO AND REPLACE NEGATIVE PATTERNS OF LIVING. RECORD WHEN YOUR DESIRES FOR THIS MERRY-GO-ROUND CHANGED AND YOU NOTICED NEW GOD-GIVEN DESIRES COMING INTO YOUR HEART.)

DATE & NOTES:

_____

_____

DATE & NOTES:

_____

_____

DATE & NOTES:

_____

_____

DATE & NOTES:

_____

_____

*Let us therefore come boldly to the throne of grace,
that we may obtain mercy and find grace to help in time of need.*
(Hebrews 4:16, NKJV)

Delight yourself in the Lord, and He will give you the desires of your heart.
(Psalm 37:4, MEV)

MY FORWARD MOVEMENT

WHAT I AM SPEAKING TO GOD ABOUT REGARDING THIS MERRY-GO-ROUND AND MY PROGRESS:

(WRITE DOWN THE DATES WHEN YOU TALKED TO GOD REGARDING THIS PARTICULAR MERRY-GO-ROUND AND WHAT YOU ASKED HIM ABOUT.)

DATE & NOTES: _____

_____

_____

DATE & NOTES: _____

_____

_____

DATE & NOTES: _____

_____

_____

DATE & NOTES: _____

_____

_____

Ask and it will be given to you; seek and you will find;
knock and it will be opened to you.
(Matthew 7:7, MEV)

MY FORWARD MOVEMENT

WHAT GOD IS SPEAKING TO ME ABOUT THIS MERRY-GO-ROUND AND MY PROGRESS:
(WRITE DOWN THE DATES WHEN YOU HEARD GOD PERSONALLY SPEAK TO YOU AND HOW HE SPECIFICALLY ANSWERED YOU ABOUT THIS PARTICULAR MERRY-GO-ROUND.)

DATE & NOTES:

_____

_____

_____

DATE & NOTES:

_____

_____

_____

DATE & NOTES:

_____

_____

_____

DATE & NOTES:

_____

_____

_____

This is what the LORD, the God of Israel says:
'Write all the words which I have spoken to you in a book."
(Jeremiah 30:2, NASB)

I'M OFF!

RECORD THE DATE WHEN YOU KNEW YOU WALKED COMPLETELY OFF THIS MERRY-GO-ROUND:

(WRITE DOWN HOW IT MAKES YOU FEEL TO BE OFF AND HOW YOU SEE YOUR LIFE NOW THAT YOU ARE NOT RIDING IT ANY LONGER. LOOK BACK IN THE SECTION WHERE YOU WROTE WHAT YOU DESIRED AND ENVISIONED THE NEW YOU TO LOOK LIKE AFTER GETTING OFF THIS MGR. DO YOU LOOK LIKE THIS NOW THAT YOU ARE OFF? I BET YOU DO!)

DATE: _____

_____

_____

_____

_____

_____

_____

_____

He also brought me up out of a horrible pit, out of the miry clay,
And set my feet upon a rock, and established my steps.
(Psalm 40:2, NKJV)

And I am convinced and sure of this very thing, that He Who began a good work in you will continue
until the day of Jesus Christ [right up to the time of His return], developing [that good work] and
perfecting and bringing it to full completion in you.
(Philippians 1:6, AMPC)

67

I AM IN THIS WORLD BUT ON MY PATH...
AVOIDING THE MERRY-GO-ROUND OF:

(ENTER THE NAME OF THIS LIFE MERRY-GO-ROUND)

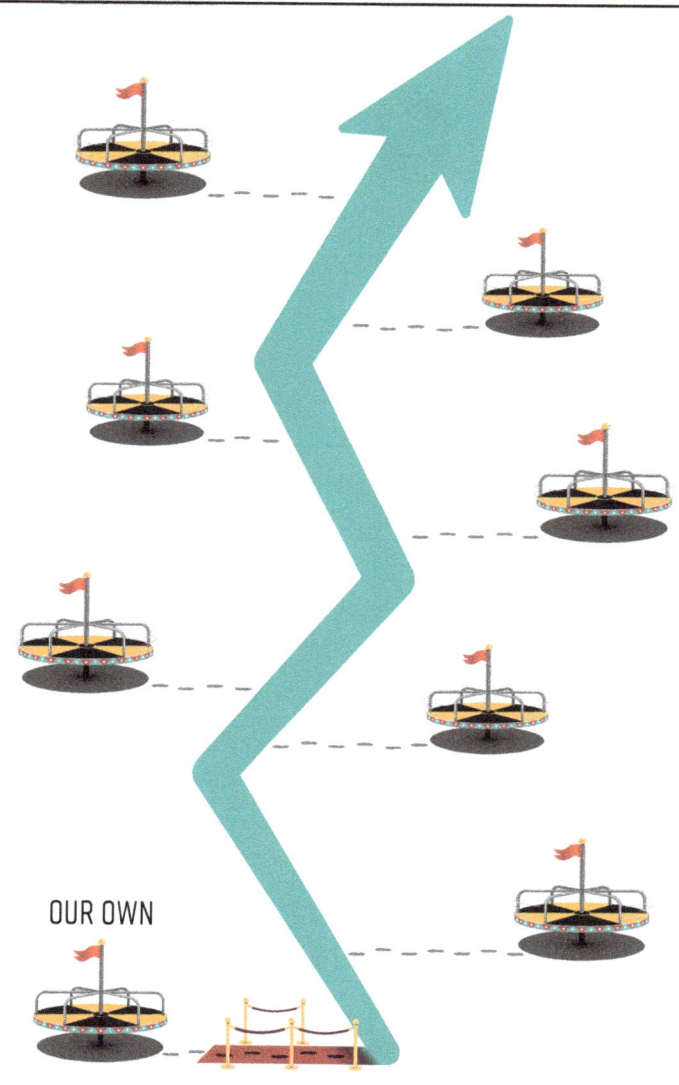

OUR OWN

Lean on, trust in, and be confident in the Lord with all your heart and mind and do not rely on your own insight or understanding. In all your ways know, recognize, and acknowledge Him, and He will direct and make straight and plain your paths.
(Proverbs 3:5-6, AMPC)

CONTINUED ACCOUNTABILITY & JOURNALING

In this section, from time to time, hold yourself accountable. Give yourself a good check-up and a reminder of where you have come from. Make sure you are still making forward progress.

Write down the dates when you come back to this workbook for review and a check-up. Journal what the thoughts, challenges, and experiences are that you have been working through.

Do you have another person holding you accountable for the progress you've made since the date you recorded getting off this merry-go-round? If so, when was it and how do they see your progress? Here are some questions to ask yourself off and on down the road: Are the old patterns of believing and acting still behind me? Am I still reaching forward to those good things which God has planned for me? (WRITE OUT PHILIPPIANS 3:13, MEV.) Am I remembering what John 5:19 says and only doing what my Good Father God leads me to do? (WRITE OUT THE VERSE.)

Be honest. Record not only your forward progress but also any relapses. Record how you got back on the merry-go-round but then got off again. Don't beat yourself up, but also don't let yourself slack off and lose the progress you worked so hard to get. You are well equipped and have been given over and above help! Regularly, take a look back at Chapters Thirteen and Fourteen in the book. It will be a good booster shot to help keep you healthy and on track! I'm cheering for you because I know that if I could do this in my life, you can do this too!

_____

_____

_____

_____

_____

_____

ON WITH YOUR life

_____

_____

_____

_____

_____

_____

_____

_____

_____

_____

_____

_____

Caleb silenced the people before Moses and said,
"Let us go up at once and possess it, for we are able to overcome it."
(Numbers 13:30, MEV)

_____

_____

_____

_____

_____

_____

_____

_____

_____

_____

_____

_____

But when anything is exposed and reproved by the light, it is made visible and clear;
and where everything is visible and clear there is light.
(Ephesians 5:13, AMPC)

OFF the Merry-Go-Round

DATE: _____

In the blank above, write THE NAME OF THE MERRY-GO-ROUND EXPOSED OR IDENTIFIED in your life. Begin with the biggest or most priority, enter the date you begin, and work through each one, revisiting this section as needed to support your progress as you get OFF the Merry-Go-Round and ON with Your Life!

COMPONENTS IDENTIFIED FOR THIS LIFE MERRY-GO-ROUND

THE CENTER POST: WHAT UNBELIEF AND LIE IS KEEPING ME ATTACHED TO THIS MERRY-GO-ROUND?

_____

WHAT FEAR IS FUELING THIS MERRY-GO-ROUND AND KEEPING IT SPINNING?

_____

THE PLATFORM/BASE: WHAT AM I DOING OVER AND OVER AGAIN THAT IS SUPPORTING THIS MERRY-GO-ROUND?

_____

DECORATIVE FIXTURES/HANDLEBARS: WHAT AM I HANGING ON TO AND LIKE SO MUCH AND DON'T WANT TO LET GO OF?

_____

THE END RESULT IF NO CHANGE IS MADE:

_____

THE END RESULT IF CHANGES ARE MADE:

_____

_____

*But clothe yourselves with the Lord Jesus Christ,
and make no provision for [nor even think about gratifying]
the flesh in regard to its improper desires.
(Romans 13:14, AMP)*

MY PERSONAL EVALUATION OF THIS LIFE MERRY-GO-ROUND

WHAT DO I LIKE ABOUT RIDING THIS MERRY-GO-ROUND?

_____

_____

WHAT DO I HATE ABOUT RIDING THIS MERRY-GO-ROUND?

_____

_____

WHY DO I WANT TO GET OFF THIS MERRY-GO-ROUND?

_____

_____

WHAT DO I SEE AS HOLDING ME BACK OR BLOCKING MY WAY FROM GOING FORWARD IN MY LIFE?

_____

_____

DO I BELIEVE I CAN GET OFF AND STAY OFF? (BE HONEST) IF NOT, EXPLAIN WHY.

_____

_____

ON THIS DAY, (INSERT THE DATE) _____

I'M CHOOSING TO STOP THE SPIN AND DO WHAT IT TAKES TO PERMANENTLY WALK OFF THIS MERRY-GO-ROUND. TODAY, I DECLARE IT, I TAKE MY FIRST STEPS OFF, AND I ENTER MY VISION OF VICTORY ON THE NEXT PAGES.

Lean on, trust in, and be confident in the Lord with all your heart and mind and do not rely on your own insight or understanding. In all your ways know, recognize, and acknowledge Him, and He will direct and make straight and plain your paths. (Proverbs 3:5-6, AMPC)

MY "RED-CARPET WALKWAY" SCRIPTURES

Sanctify them by Your truth. Your word is truth.
(John 17:17)

I'M BELIEVING & CONFESSING TO PROGRESSIVELY RENEW MY MIND USING THESE SCRIPTURES:
(YOU CAN ADD MORE ALONG THE WAY.)

1. _____

2. _____

3. _____

4. _____

5. _____

6. _____

7. _____

8. _____

9. _____

10. _____

11. _____

Your word is a lamp to my feet
And a light to my path.
(Psalm 119:105, NKJV)

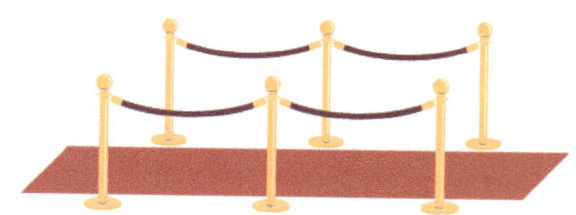

MY FORWARD MOVEMENT

WHAT I DESIRE THE NEW ME TO LOOK LIKE:
THE IMAGE I WANT TO HAVE OF MYSELF OFF THIS LIFE MERRY-GO-ROUND

_____

_____

THE DESIRES IN MY HEART I WANT TO SEE COME TO PASS:

_____

_____

HOW I WANT MY RELATIONSHIP WITH GOD TO LOOK:

_____

_____

HOW I WANT MY CHANGED LIFE TO HELP OTHERS:

_____

_____

_____

_____

He sends forth His word and heals them and
rescues them from the pit and destruction.
(Psalm 107:20, AMPC)

MY FORWARD MOVEMENT

MY THOUGHTS OF MYSELF ARE BEGINNING TO LOOK LIKE GOD'S THOUGHTS FOR ME!
(RECORD ALL THE TIMES YOU NOTICE THOUGHTS OF YOURSELF CHANGING TO LINE UP AND AGREE WITH GOD'S GOOD THOUGHTS OF YOU.)

DATE & NOTES:

_____

_____

_____

DATE & NOTES:

_____

_____

_____

DATE & NOTES:

_____

_____

_____

DATE & NOTES:

_____

_____

_____

*For I know the thoughts that I think toward you, says the LORD,
thoughts of peace and not of evil, to give you a future and a hope.
(Jeremiah 29:11, NKJV)*

MY FORWARD MOVEMENT

I'M TAKING DIFFERENT ACTIONS!

(RECORD THE DATES WHEN YOU OR SOMEONE ELSE NOTICES YOU TAKING DIFFERENT ACTIONS BECAUSE YOU ARE ALLOWING CHRIST AND YOUR NEW NATURE IN HIM TO MOVE YOU FORWARD INTO A NEW WAY OF LIVING.)

DATE & NOTES:

_____

_____

_____

DATE & NOTES:

_____

_____

_____

DATE & NOTES:

_____

_____

_____

DATE & NOTES:

_____

_____

_____

I have been crucified with Christ [in Him I have shared His crucifixion]; it is no longer I who live, but Christ (the Messiah) lives in me; and the life I now live in the body I live by faith in (by adherence to and reliance on and complete trust in) the Son of God, Who loved me and gave Himself up for me.
(Galatians 2:20, AMPC)

MY FORWARD MOVEMENT

THE IMAGE I HAVE OF MYSELF IS CHANGING TO THE IMAGE I AM IN CHRIST!
(RECORD THE DATES WHEN YOU REALIZE THE IMAGE YOU HAVE OF YOURSELF IS CHANGING AND BECOMING RENEWED TO WHO YOU ARE ON THE INSIDE AS A BORN-AGAIN BELIEVER IN CHRIST JESUS.)

DATE & NOTES:

_____

_____

_____

DATE & NOTES:

_____

_____

_____

DATE & NOTES:

_____

_____

_____

DATE & NOTES:

_____

_____

_____

*Though our outer man is [progressively] decaying and wasting away,
yet our inner self is being [progressively] renewed day after day.
(2 Corinthians 4:16b, AMPC)*

MY FORWARD MOVEMENT

I'M RESISTING URGES TO GO BACK TO MY OLD WAY OF LIVING!

(RECORD THE DATES WHEN YOU MADE A STAND AND DEMANDED CHANGE TO COME, RESISTING AN URGE TO GO BACK INTO YOUR OLD WAYS OF DOING THINGS. WRITE DOWN IF SOMEONE ELSE NOTICED IT ALSO.)

DATE & NOTES: _____

_____

_____

DATE & NOTES: _____

_____

_____

DATE & NOTES: _____

_____

_____

DATE & NOTES: _____

_____

_____

But He gives more grace. For this reason it says:
"God resists the proud, but gives grace to the humble."
Therefore submit yourselves to God. Resist the devil, and he will flee from you.
(James 4:6-7, MEV)

MY FORWARD MOVEMENT

I AM REPLACING THIS MERRY-GO-ROUND DECORATION AND DESIRES WITH:

(RECORD EACH TIME WHEN AND HOW YOU USED GOD'S GRACE TO HELP YOU LET GO AND REPLACE NEGATIVE PATTERNS OF LIVING. RECORD WHEN YOUR DESIRES FOR THIS MERRY-GO-ROUND CHANGED AND YOU NOTICED NEW GOD-GIVEN DESIRES COMING INTO YOUR HEART.)

DATE & NOTES: _____

_____

_____

DATE & NOTES: _____

_____

_____

DATE & NOTES: _____

_____

_____

DATE & NOTES: _____

_____

_____

Let us therefore come boldly to the throne of grace,
that we may obtain mercy and find grace to help in time of need.
(Hebrews 4:16, NKJV)

Delight yourself in the Lord, and He will give you the desires of your heart.
(Psalm 37:4, MEV)

MY FORWARD MOVEMENT

WHAT I AM SPEAKING TO GOD ABOUT REGARDING THIS MERRY-GO-ROUND AND MY PROGRESS:
(WRITE DOWN THE DATES WHEN YOU TALKED TO GOD REGARDING THIS PARTICULAR MERRY-GO-ROUND AND WHAT YOU ASKED HIM ABOUT.)

DATE & NOTES:

_____

_____

DATE & NOTES:

_____

_____

DATE & NOTES:

_____

_____

DATE & NOTES:

_____

_____

Ask and it will be given to you; seek and you will find;
knock and it will be opened to you.
(Matthew 7:7, MEV)

MY FORWARD MOVEMENT

WHAT GOD IS SPEAKING TO ME ABOUT THIS MERRY-GO-ROUND AND MY PROGRESS:
(WRITE DOWN THE DATES WHEN YOU HEARD GOD PERSONALLY SPEAK TO YOU AND HOW HE SPECIFICALLY ANSWERED YOU ABOUT THIS PARTICULAR MERRY-GO-ROUND.)

DATE & NOTES:

_____

_____

_____

DATE & NOTES:

_____

_____

_____

DATE & NOTES:

_____

_____

_____

DATE & NOTES:

_____

_____

_____

This is what the LORD, the God of Israel says:
'Write all the words which I have spoken to you in a book."
(Jeremiah 30:2, NASB)

I'M OFF!

RECORD THE DATE WHEN YOU KNEW YOU WALKED COMPLETELY OFF THIS MERRY-GO-ROUND:

(WRITE DOWN HOW IT MAKES YOU FEEL TO BE OFF AND HOW YOU SEE YOUR LIFE NOW THAT YOU ARE NOT RIDING IT ANY LONGER. LOOK BACK IN THE SECTION WHERE YOU WROTE WHAT YOU DESIRED AND ENVISIONED THE NEW YOU TO LOOK LIKE AFTER GETTING OFF THIS MGR. DO YOU LOOK LIKE THIS NOW THAT YOU ARE OFF? I BET YOU DO!)

DATE: _____

_____

_____

_____

_____

_____

_____

_____

He also brought me up out of a horrible pit, out of the miry clay,
And set my feet upon a rock, and established my steps.
(Psalm 40:2, NKJV)

And I am convinced and sure of this very thing, that He Who began a good work in you will continue
until the day of Jesus Christ [right up to the time of His return], developing [that good work] and
perfecting and bringing it to full completion in you.
(Philippians 1:6, AMPC)

I AM IN THIS WORLD BUT ON MY PATH...
AVOIDING THE MERRY-GO-ROUND OF:

(ENTER THE NAME OF THIS LIFE MERRY-GO-ROUND)

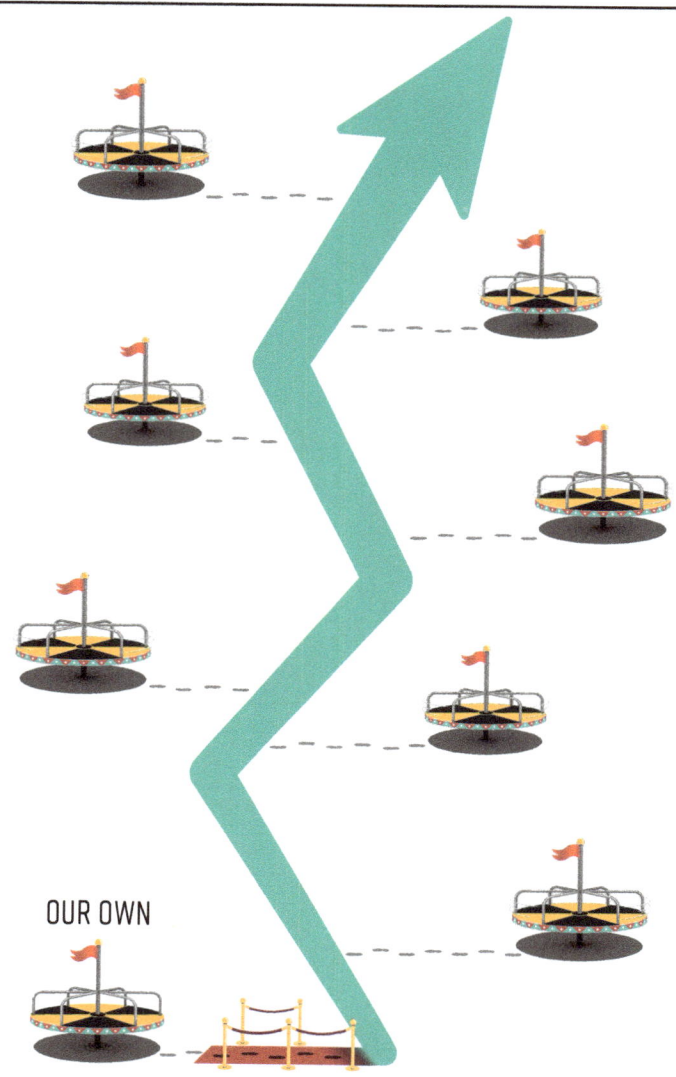

OUR OWN

Lean on, trust in, and be confident in the Lord with all your heart and mind and do not rely on your own insight or understanding. In all your ways know, recognize, and acknowledge Him, and He will direct and make straight and plain your paths.
(Proverbs 3:5-6, AMPC)

CONTINUED ACCOUNTABILITY & JOURNALING

In this section, from time to time, hold yourself accountable. Give yourself a good check-up and a reminder of where you have come from. Make sure you are still making forward progress.

Write down the dates when you come back to this workbook for review and a check-up. Journal what the thoughts, challenges, and experiences are that you have been working through.

Do you have another person holding you accountable for the progress you've made since the date you recorded getting off this merry-go-round? If so, when was it and how do they see your progress? Here are some questions to ask yourself off and on down the road: Are the old patterns of believing and acting still behind me? Am I still reaching forward to those good things which God has planned for me? (WRITE OUT PHILIPPIANS 3:13, MEV.) Am I remembering what John 5:19 says and only doing what my Good Father God leads me to do? (WRITE OUT THE VERSE.)

Be honest. Record not only your forward progress but also any relapses. Record how you got back on the merry-go-round but then got off again. Don't beat yourself up, but also don't let yourself slack off and lose the progress you worked so hard to get. You are well equipped and have been given over and above help! Regularly, take a look back at Chapters Thirteen and Fourteen in the book. It will be a good booster shot to help keep you healthy and on track! I'm cheering for you because I know that if I could do this in my life, you can do this too!

_____

_____

_____

_____

_____

_____

_____

_____

_____

_____

_____

_____

_____

_____

_____

_____

_____

_____

_____

Caleb silenced the people before Moses and said,
"Let us go up at once and possess it, for we are able to overcome it."
(Numbers 13:30, MEV)

ON
WITH YOUR
life

_____

_____

_____

_____

_____

_____

_____

_____

_____

_____

But when anything is exposed and reproved by the light, it is made visible and clear;
and where everything is visible and clear there is light.
(Ephesians 5:13, AMPC)

Meet the Author:
Dana Marie Ecklund

Author. Speaker. Teacher. Businesswoman. Friend. Whatever role or venue you meet her in, you will soon discover that Dana's biggest desire is to lead people to Jesus and help them see who they are as born-again believers. She is a cheerleader at heart and loves seeing people get off circumstantial merry-go-rounds and on to the path God has for them in this life.

Here's a lady who has gone through numerous trials and tribulations and has remained faithful, not just months or weeks, but for years. Her faith has been displayed and defined throughout her 38 years of marriage as she and her husband raised four children amidst impossible situations. Her various life experiences, which took her on one merry-go-round after another, cover the following areas and more: religious legalism, sexual identity crises, pornography, sexual abuse, family members who struggled with substance abuse lifestyles (including prison and rehab time), her own marriage struggles, children with major health diagnoses, work, school, and more.

Through all of these things, Dana has proven that she can recognize merry-go-rounds and is not afraid to get off and go forward. No matter the circumstances or situations she faced, she never quit believing God and His Word. She held to the Word of God. It has been her Rock. It is evident that her foundation, who is the Lord Jesus Christ, is strong! This is who she is, and her victories are fully displayed in her life.

In 2017, Dana and her husband, David, jumped off the merry-go-round of frustration caused by not moving forward into their hearts' desires. As they finally stepped out to follow God's plan for their lives together, they attended Charis Bible College in Woodland Park, CO, on campus for the next three years. Dana graduated her third year from the Charis Business School, and David from the Charis Practical Government School, in May 2020. Determined to keep moving forward, she is building the business God dropped in her heart in 2015. She is also helping her husband express his God-given passions through his Good News teachings of the true Gospel of Jesus Christ and the Church's role in culture.

Dana and David Ecklund began their marriage in Southern California in 1983. They moved to raise their family in the mid-west and are now back in Southern California. Dana is a mother of three daughters, one son, and a grandmother of seven so far.

To invite Dana Marie Ecklund to speak,
to find additional products and motivational tools, or
to purchase additional copies, please visit :

OnWithYourLife.com